Photo by Suzanne N. Plunkett

John Judd and Kate Goerhing in a scene from the Victory Gardens Theater production of "Drowning Sorrows." Set design by Bill Bartelt.

DROWNING SORROWS

BY DOUGLAS POST

★

★

DRAMATISTS
PLAY SERVICE
INC.

2

This play is dedicated to Lloyd Richards who always holds a mirror up to nature.

DROWNING SORROWS received its world premiere at the Victory Gardens Theater (Dennis Zacek, Artistic Director) in Chicago, Illinois, on November 8, 1996. It was directed by Curt Columbus; the set design was by Bill Bartelt; the costume design was by Margaret Morettini; the lighting design was by David Gipson; the sound design was by Lindsay Jones; and the production stage manager was Shane Spaulding. The cast was as follows:

COLE RUCKER ....Kenn E. Head
DUNCAN CRAWFORD..John Judd
GINA FRANCES ....Keli Garrett
RAYMOND MILES ....Andrew Leman
EMILY MILES ....Kate Goerhing

DROWNING SORROWS had previously been produced as a live-in-performance radio show as a part of the series Chicago Theatres On The Air in Chicago, Illinois, on April 1, 1996. It was directed by Curt Columbus. The cast was as follows:

COLE RUCKER..Paul Winfield
DUNCAN CRAWFORD ....Harry Hamlin
GINA FRANCES ....Keli Garrett
RAYMOND MILES ....Andrew Leman
EMILY MILES ....Martha Lavey

DROWNING SORROWS was presented as a staged reading at the American Soviet Theater Initiative's 1995 Shelykova Play-wrights Conference in Shelykova, Russia on June 14, 1995. It was directed by Tina Ball; the translation was by Tamara Arapova. The cast was as follows:

COLE RUCKER..Igor Tchurikov
DUNCAN CRAWFORD ....Vadim Raikin
GINA FRANCES ....Tatianna Konductorova
RAYMOND MILES ....Yevgenny Dorgov
EMILY MILES ....Julia Perova

DROWNING SORROWS was originally presented as a staged reading at the 1994 National Playwrights Conference (Lloyd Richards, Artistic Director) at the Eugene O'Neill Theater Center in Waterford, Connecticut, on July 9, 1994. It was directed by Tina Ball; the dramaturg was Philip Barry; the set design was by G. W. Mercer; the lighting design was by Spencer Mosse; the production stage manager was Tom Aberger. The cast was as follows:

COLE RUCKER ....Tommy Hollis
DUNCAN CRAWFORD ....Sam McMurray
GINA FRANCES ....Linda Maurel Sithole
RAYMOND MILES ....William Wise
EMILY MILES...Katherine Borowitz

CHARACTERS

COLE RUCKER, a fisherman, late 40s
DUNCAN CRAWFORD, a bartender, early 40s
GINA FRANCES, a waitress, late 20s
RAYMOND MILES, an investment banker, early 50s
EMILY MILES, an heiress, late 30s

TIME

Summer.

PLACE

A bar on the east end of the island of St. John.

DROWNING SORROWS should be performed without an intermission.

DROWNING SORROWS

SCENE ONE

A bar on the east end of the island of St. John. The place is made up entirely of wood. A wooden floor. Wooden beams and rafters. Wooden tables and chairs. And everything is weathered. The open walls are filled with the greenery of the island. A doorway to one side leads out onto a deck and then down onto a beach. The sound of the water rises and falls with the action of the play. It is summer. Early afternoon. Sunlight pours into the room. The tables are littered with empty glasses. The ashtrays are filled. The floor is dirty. Duncan, who is white and originally from the States, stands behind the bar, shuffling a deck of cards. He deals himself five, looks at them, puts them back in the deck, reshuffles, and repeats the process. Cole, who is black and a native of the island, sits at the bar drinking a shot and a beer.

COLE.   Did I ever tell you the story of how I lost my wife?
DUNCAN.   I believe you have.
COLE.   The story of how I came to be a single man?
DUNCAN.   I think so.
COLE.   The man I am today?
DUNCAN.   Yes.
COLE.   Well, then. *(Pause.)* We were on a boat. My boat. The boat that sits docked down there on the beach. One and the very same. I was younger then. And stronger. And a better fisherman than I am today. At least I had a hunger for it then. At least it was still something of an adventure. So. She and I, we were out there on the water. On holiday. Our holiday. And we'd been drinking. And suddenly the weather turned. The

wind it picked up and the sky went dark. But we did not pay it any mind. Why? We were happy. Everything was fine. And she was laughing. At me. At something I'd said. And then the boat heeled over. And I reached for the rail and caught hold of it. And then I reached for her. And I missed. And she was still laughing. Laughing even as my hand went out and could not reach her. And then she went over the side of the boat. She simply lost her footing and fell. I did not know what to do. I dived into the water. Down in after her. And the rain started to fall with a great force. It came gushing out of the sky. And the wind it was gusting now and fierce. But I could not find her. I knew she was there. Somewhere near me in the water. But I could not see her. Or get to her. Then it was too late. Then it was all I could do to swim to shore, out of breath, and shouting out for someone to help me. To help us. But there was no help. No one to do anything. It was over. And all because of this: *(Pause.)* I reached for the rail. I reached for the rail before I reached for her. I should have reached for her first.

DUNCAN. Then you would have both drowned.

COLE. Sorry?

DUNCAN. I said, then you would have both gone under. The two of you. Together.

COLE. What do you mean?

DUNCAN. Well, it stands to reason, doesn't it? I mean, if you'd reached for her and then reached for the rail, she would have pulled you over.

COLE. Yes, but —

DUNCAN. Her weight would have pulled you down. And out. And into the water.

COLE. Here's the thing —

DUNCAN. It's the law of nature. It's nothing against you. Against what you could have done.

COLE. Or should have done.

DUNCAN. It's just the way things are.

COLE. But —

8

DUNCAN. You saved yourself.

COLE. Yes, but —

DUNCAN. You couldn't save her, too.

COLE. I should have tried.

DUNCAN. Maybe.

COLE. That's all I'm saying, man. It's that simple. I should have reached for her first.

DUNCAN. Let me tell you something.

COLE. What?

DUNCAN. Nothing in this life is that simple.

COLE. No?

DUNCAN. No. We all have our regrets.

COLE. We do?

DUNCAN. Oh, yes.

COLE. And what do you regret?

DUNCAN. Me?

COLE. I am asking.

DUNCAN. Well. *(He laughs.)* I regret that I'm here. Stuck behind this bar on a day like this. With a wind in the air. And the water almost calm. I would love to be somewhere else.

COLE. Where?

DUNCAN. Anywhere. *(He pushes the deck aside, goes to the door, and looks out.)* On a boat. At sea. Further south in the Caribbean. Or farther still. Where a man could breathe. Where he could begin again. As somebody else.

COLE. Like who? *(Duncan shrugs.)*

DUNCAN. Oh, I don't know. Maybe a sailor. Or a painter. Or a poet. A politician. An entrepreneur. *(He laughs.)* I mean, don't you ever wonder?

COLE. What?

DUNCAN. If maybe our life isn't out there somewhere? In the form of some ... grand adventure? Waiting to happen?

COLE. No.

DUNCAN. No?

COLE. Never. Anyway, you and I, we are not talking about the same thing.

DUNCAN. We're not?

COLE. You are talking about another life. Something in your head. A picture of what could be. I am talking about what has been. What is part of me. Like an arm. Or a leg. Something I can never lose. That will always be with me. I am talking about *this* life. *This* one. *Here*. *(Gina, who is black and also originally from the States, enters the bar.)* I should have reached for her first.

GINA. Hello, Cole.

COLE. Gina.

GINA. Nothing biting?

COLE. Not today. I have been working the deep wells around Hurricane Bay every morning for a week now and the fish they go out of their way to make fun. They swim around the boat making faces. Looking up at me like I am a great fool. A clown. Or worse. With pity.

GINA. Well, I'm sorry to hear it. *(She hands a stack of business cards to Duncan.)* These are for you.

DUNCAN. What are they?

GINA. What do they look like?

DUNCAN. They look like cards. Business cards. With my name on them.

COLE. Let me see. *(Duncan hands Cole a card.)* "Duncan's Saloon. On the east end of St. John. Stop in for a friendly drink." I wonder.

GINA. What?

COLE. Can a drink really be friendly? *(Gina sees the state of the room, the empty glasses, the ashtrays, the general mess, and starts cleaning.)*

DUNCAN. Where did you get these?

GINA. I had them printed up.

DUNCAN. Why?

GINA. Well, I had this wild idea that they might actually get us some customers.

DUNCAN. I see. All right, then. I'll take them with me the

next time I go into town.

GINA.   I already gave a stack to Simon.

DUNCAN.   You ... you gave them to the boy?

GINA.   Yes.

DUNCAN.   Why?

GINA.   So he can hand them out.

DUNCAN.   Where?

GINA.   At the docks.

DUNCAN.   In town?

GINA.   Yes, of course, in town.

DUNCAN.   Wait now, wait a minute, you're telling me that boy of yours is standing down at the docks handing out these cards to total strangers?

GINA.   To tourists, Duncan.

DUNCAN.   Well, I don't want him to.

GINA.   Why not?

DUNCAN.   Because I don't want him working for me.

GINA.   He's not working for you. He's happy to do it. He likes the idea.

DUNCAN.   Look, Gina, I appreciate the effort, I do, but the last thing I want is you and your son attempting to draw a crowd into my establishment.

GINA.   A crowd? (*She laughs.*) Duncan, we're lucky to get two or three people in here on a given afternoon.

DUNCAN.   Yes, well, that's plenty.

GINA.   It is certainly *not* plenty.

DUNCAN.   It is certainly *near* plenty *if* they spend enough money.

GINA.   They never spend enough money. Not on us. They spend it on the four-star hotel in town with hot tubs and tennis courts.

DUNCAN.   Gina —

GINA.   What?

DUNCAN.   It's too early in the day to argue.

GINA.   It is never too early. (*Cole stands up.*)

11

COLE. Well now, I think I'll go down and wash off that boat of mine.

DUNCAN. Oh, yes?

COLE. Yes. I can't sit here all day drinking your whiskey. Much as I'd like to. Much as I'd rather be doing almost anything than tending to work. I'll come by later and we'll play a game.

DUNCAN. Cards?

COLE. No, not cards. You always kill me at cards. Maybe dominoes.

DUNCAN. All right.

COLE. Yes, dominoes. I like dominoes. Do you know why?

DUNCAN. Let me guess.

COLE. Because there are less numbers to be counted. Less rules to remember. And so fewer mistakes to be made. *(He exits.)*

GINA. And therefore more whiskey to be consumed.

DUNCAN. Yes.

GINA. Which you will put on his tab.

DUNCAN. Probably.

GINA. Which he will never pay.

DUNCAN. No, I doubt that he ever will.

GINA. Your friend, Cole, is one sad drunk of a man.

DUNCAN. He's your friend, too.

GINA. Not when he drinks like this. Not when he can barely stand up. Why do you let him do it?

DUNCAN. Do what?

GINA. Why do you continue to feed him alcohol when you know all it does is produce that story in him?

DUNCAN. The one about his wife. Drowning. The way she did.

GINA. What does it do for him? To say it over and over and over again?

DUNCAN. Well, it's his moment.

GINA. His what?

DUNCAN.   His moment of definition.

GINA.   What do you mean?

DUNCAN.   It defines him. It tells him what he is. What he's made of.

GINA.   What are you talking about?

DUNCAN.   The man knows, Gina. He knows what he's capable of doing. Or not doing. *(Pause.)* He knows who he is. *(He sits at a table. A moment. Then Gina comes up behind him. She puts her arms around him. She kisses him.)*

GINA.   I missed you last night.

DUNCAN.   Oh, yes?

GINA.   Yes. *(She kisses him again.)* Did you miss me?

DUNCAN.   I did.

GINA.   Oh, really?

DUNCAN.   Really.

GINA.   Well, then show me. *(She continues touching him.)* Show me how much you missed me.

DUNCAN.   Gina —

GINA.   Yes?

DUNCAN.   What if somebody walks in?

GINA.   Like who?

DUNCAN.   Clientele.

GINA.   We'll charge them extra. *(She continues.)* Show me. *(Duncan pulls her down onto his lap and kisses her deeply. His hands move over her body. She laughs and looks at him.)* Well, now I believe you. *(He laughs.)* So what's happening?

DUNCAN.   What do you mean?

GINA.   I mean, it's been almost a week now.

DUNCAN.   A week?

GINA.   Since you've been by the house.

DUNCAN.   No.

GINA.   Yes. *(Pause.)* Last Saturday night you said that you had business to take care of.

DUNCAN.   I did.

GINA.   And then Sunday it was inventory.

13

DUNCAN. Yes, well, it was.

GINA. And then Monday, Tuesday, Wednesday, I waited up for you, but you never showed. And then last night, well, I guess I was surprised. I thought for sure you'd be coming by.

DUNCAN. Why?

GINA. You don't remember?

DUNCAN. What? *(Pause.)* His birthday. *(Pause.)* It was Simon's birthday. Oh, God. Gina, I am so sorry.

GINA. It's all right.

DUNCAN. No, no, I completely forgot.

GINA. I can tell.

DUNCAN. Why didn't you remind me?

GINA. Why? *(She laughs, gets up, and moves away from him.)* Because I don't want to start sounding like a wife, Duncan. I don't want to be reminding you of things. If you remember, you remember.

DUNCAN. I'll make it up to him.

GINA. Don't worry about it.

DUNCAN. No, I'll rent a boat. We'll go sailing.

GINA. Don't.

DUNCAN. Snorkeling.

GINA. Duncan —

DUNCAN. We'll make a day of it.

GINA. Listen to me! *(Pause.)* You don't owe us anything. *(Pause.)* You don't. *(Pause.)* I knew it was a gamble that first night when I asked you home for dinner. But I always liked you. I liked being here with you. Working with you. It felt like we were building something together. A bar. A friendship. And I knew you weren't seeing any of those so-called girlfriends of yours at the time.

DUNCAN. Now what do you mean by that?

GINA. You know what I mean. *(Pause.)* So I asked you home because I thought it might be nice. *(Pause.)* And it was. *(Pause.)* Wasn't it?

DUNCAN. Yes. Yes, it was more than nice. It was, um ... mean-

14

ingful. *(She laughs.)*

GINA. And the next day we got up and made breakfast and Simon came into the kitchen and saw you sitting there like it was the most natural thing in the world. And we walked him to school and came here and opened up the bar. And neither of us said a word about it. But I knew you'd be coming home with me again that night. And the night after that. And the night after that.

DUNCAN. It just sort of ... happened.

GINA. Uh-huh.

DUNCAN. I mean, we never really talked it through.

GINA. We never did.

DUNCAN. Well. *(Pause.)* I don't know what to say. *(Pause.)* I mean, these last few months ... what's it been now? Four, five?

GINA. Six.

DUNCAN. No.

GINA. Yes. *(She smiles.)* Not that I'm counting.

DUNCAN. Six months. *(He laughs.)* God, I'd love to know where the days go. *(Pause.)* Anyway, it's been ... good. Being with you. And the boy. It's been easy. Comfortable.

GINA. So what's wrong?

DUNCAN. Nothing's wrong.

GINA. Because if it's another woman —

DUNCAN. No.

GINA. You can tell me.

DUNCAN. It's not that.

GINA. I won't fall apart.

DUNCAN. Believe me, it's not another woman.

GINA. Then what? *(Pause.)* Where were you last night?

DUNCAN. I was here. At the bar. Working.

GINA. Working?

DUNCAN. Yes. *(Pause.)* Do you remember that crew that was in here a few days ago? The men who've been sailing together for the better part of six months?

GINA. The ones from Britain? And France?

15

DUNCAN. Right. Well, they told me that they might stop by for drinks. And a game of cards.

GINA. Cards?

DUNCAN. For money. *(Pause.)* At first I only watched, but then they invited me to play and I thought, well, what the hell, I need the income. The bank's been beating on my door about catching up on those payments. And then there's the back salary I owe you.

GINA. I don't care about that.

DUNCAN. I do. And these guys were throwing hundred dollar bills around the table like they were match sticks. So I said yes. And then after it was over, after they'd cleared out, it was almost four A.M. So I slept here.

GINA. On that cot of yours in the storeroom.

DUNCAN. Well, what's wrong with that? It's my property, isn't it? My home?

GINA. It's not a home, Duncan. Not a real one. *(Pause.)* So how did you do?

DUNCAN. At cards?

GINA. Yes.

DUNCAN. I cleaned up. Collected enough cash to pay off my debts. Including you. *(He reaches into his pocket, pulls out a wad of bills, and hands most of them to her.)*

GINA. No, it's all right, I don't —

DUNCAN. Take it. *(She does. A moment. She looks at the money in her hand.)* I still have a few dollars left to cover me for a week or two.

GINA. Until there's another game.

DUNCAN. Yes. *(Pause.)* Or until something else happens.

GINA. Like what?

DUNCAN. Well.... *(Pause.)* Those men, the ones who were in here last night, lost their second mate to a woman on Cozumel.

GINA. And?

DUNCAN. And they're preparing to set sail tomorrow. They're going down to Belize. And then Brazil. And then out

16

across the South Atlantic. And onto the tip of Africa.

GINA.   I'm listening.

DUNCAN.   And they've asked me to go along.

GINA.   They — ?

DUNCAN.   Invited me to join them. Even though I suspect the reason has less to do with the pleasure of my company and more with the possibility of winning their money back. Of which there's almost nothing left.

GINA.   You're going with them?

DUNCAN.   I would. If I could. If I had the resources. I'd have to cover my own expenses. And supplies. Which at the moment I can't do. So unless I can locate some sort of high stakes game in the next twenty-four hours the possibility seems … remote.

GINA.   You'd actually go?

DUNCAN.   I'd come back.

GINA.   Who'd take care of the bar?

DUNCAN.   You. Cole.

GINA.   Cole? *(She laughs.)* He can barely take care of himself. As for me, don't count on anything.

DUNCAN.   Gina —

GINA.   What?

DUNCAN.   See, now I knew you wouldn't take this well.

GINA.   Are you seriously considering this?

DUNCAN.   Yes! *(Pause.)* Yes, because apart from everything else, I am slowly going crazy on this goddamn island! *(Pause.)* One of the guys last night, this Brit, asked me how long I'd been here and I had to think for a moment before I could say. Seventeen years. Seventeen years of listening to the same people. Of hearing the same stories. Of walking the same road that circles the perimeters and always, always coming back to the same place. Yes, it's a beautiful place. I'll give you that. But I feel like the life is draining out of me. Like my head's filled with sand and my brain's been eaten up by the sun. I mean, the repetition, the sheer repetition of it all, when there's this part of me that never gets used, that actually had aspirations, once upon a time.

GINA.   To do what?

DUNCAN.   Oh, I don't know. See the world, I guess. And maybe figure out a thing or two. Like what is it that I'm doing here. What I'm meant to be about. Besides this. This bar. These people. This piece of rock. *(Pause.)* I have to get off the island, Gina. Even for a brief period of time. A … month or two at most.

GINA.   I see. *(Pause.)* So that's what you've been working at.

DUNCAN.   What?

GINA.   A way out.

DUNCAN.   No.

GINA.   A way to get away.

DUNCAN.   I never —

GINA.   Because when it comes right down to it all I really am is just another somebody who comes into this bar every day with a story you're tired of hearing.

DUNCAN.   Now you know that's not the case.

GINA.   Then what am I? *(Pause.)* To you? What am I to you? *(Pause.)* Am I your employee? Your coworker? Your cocktail waitress? *(Pause.)* Am I your woman? *(Pause.)* Am I someone to lie down with? Someone to tell your sorrows to? To see in the new day? *(Pause.)* Am I your friend? A skirt to flirt with? A body that you sometimes fall into? *(Pause.)* What am I?

DUNCAN.   Well. *(Pause.)* I don't know that I can answer in a word.

GINA.   Then use two. *(Pause.)* I'm telling you, Duncan, if you do this, if you go away with these men, these foreigners, I won't be here when you get back.

DUNCAN.   Gina —

GINA.   Not the way I am now.

DUNCAN.   Please, don't —

GINA.   Because it's not just me anymore. It's Simon, too. I've got to think about him. What it means to have you come and go. I have to. *(Pause.)* It's all right. We'll go back to the way it was before. But we can't be lovers. Not like this. Not with one foot in the door and the other out to sea. *(Pause.)* It has to be one way or the other. *(A moment. Then Cole enters.)*

COLE. You've got customers out on the deck. Two people with money to spend. I can smell it. *(Pause.)*

GINA. I'll go. *(She exits. Cole sits.)*

COLE. Did I ever tell you that I named the boat after her?

DUNCAN. Who?

COLE. My wife.

DUNCAN. Oh. *(Pause.)* No.

COLE. I did. That day. When we were out to sea. Celebrating. I christened the boat in her name. In honor of her laughter. I broke a bottle on the hull and said I would paint her name there as soon as we got back. And then that sudden change of weather. And the loss of her. And later when they brought the boat back to me, and her no longer with it, I could do nothing. Could only stare at the empty shell of a thing. And the place where her name would have been. Or should have been. The place where she no longer was.

DUNCAN. Cole?

COLE. Yes?

DUNCAN. I thought you were going to wash down your skiff.

COLE. I was, I was, I — *(Pause.)* Got lost in that moment. *(Gina enters.)*

GINA. Chivas on the rocks and a vodka martini, no olive. *(Duncan goes about mixing the drinks.)*

COLE. The thing is I can't forget. Her. The memory of her. Of our time together. Then. As husband and wife. Her laughter. The way she laughed at me. At something I'd said. I wish I could remember what it was. What it was that made her laugh that day.

GINA. And what would she think of you now?

DUNCAN. Gina —

GINA. What would this woman, this wife of yours, this memory think of a man who spends most of his waking hours in a

19

state of immobility?

DUNCAN. Don't.

COLE. She — *(Pause.)* Would understand.

GINA. Then she was an exceptional woman. Then you've got every right to mourn her. *(Pause.)* But I think you're only fooling yourself. *(Raymond, who is white and originally from England, enters the bar and stands in the doorway.)*

RAYMOND. I'm sorry to bother you, but would it be possible for us to have our drinks in here?

GINA. Of course.

RAYMOND. It's so much cooler, you see. So much more pleasant. And I'm afraid that my wife is feeling ill.

GINA. Is there anything we can do?

RAYMOND. No, no, it is nothing. It will pass. I simply need to get her out of the sun.

DUNCAN. Come inside.

RAYMOND. Thank you so much. *(He exits.)*

COLE. What do you mean?

GINA. What?

COLE. What can you know of it?

GINA. I know what I know.

COLE. And what is that? No. Nothing. A man is the sum of his parts. His experiences. And to think that he can cut them loose, leave them behind like some old baggage, no, it cannot be done.

DUNCAN. Cole —

COLE. It is not possible.

DUNCAN. She didn't mean anything by it.

COLE. I know what she meant. She meant I should forget. Well, I'd like to. Believe me, woman, I would love to. But the thing is I can't.

GINA. I'm sorry I brought it up.

COLE. I simply....

GINA. I'm sorry, Cole.

COLE. Cannot. *(Emily, who is white and from the States, enters the*

20

bar with Raymond.)

DUNCAN. Sit anywhere you like.

RAYMOND. Again, thank you. *(They sit.)* We've been traveling all day, you see. Since five o'clock this morning. First the flight to Puerto Rico. Then a connecting flight to St. Thomas. Then a limousine ride to the ferry. The ferry to the island. And, finally, checking in at the hotel.

DUNCAN. You must be tired.

RAYMOND. Yes, we are. But, for some inexplicable reason, neither one of us could sit still. And so we decide to rent a car. We set out. We are told that it is next to impossible to get lost on the island.

DUNCAN. Yes.

RAYMOND. That there is only the one road.

DUNCAN. That's right.

RAYMOND. And still somehow we manage to make a wrong turn. We are temporarily misplaced. And then my wife remembers. A boy. At the side of the dock. With a smile to welcome us. And a card. *(He pulls it out.)* Duncan's Saloon.

DUNCAN. Well, there you are. *(He looks at Gina. She smiles. He serves them their drinks.)* Or, rather, here you are.

RAYMOND. Indeed.

DUNCAN. Your drinks.

RAYMOND. Many thanks.

DUNCAN. Chivas. *(Raymond takes his glass and raises it.)*

RAYMOND. To your health.

DUNCAN. And a vodka martini. *(Emily reaches for her glass. She looks up at Duncan. She stops.)*

RAYMOND. My dear, are you all right?

EMILY. Yes, I'm fine. Really. I — *(She attempts to stand up. She falters. Then she simply collapses on the floor. They all go to her. They gather around.)*

RAYMOND. Emily?

EMILY. I'm all right.

DUNCAN. Is she — ?

21

EMILY. Really.

RAYMOND. I don't know.

GINA. Maybe some water.

EMILY. No, I —

COLE. Help her up.

EMILY. No, really, if I could only sit here for a moment.

RAYMOND. My love — ?

EMILY. *(She shouts.)* A moment! Please! I'm all right! *(Silence. They stare down at her. She looks up at them.)* I really am all right.

SCENE TWO

Late afternoon. Raymond stands in the doorway staring out with a drink in his hand. Emily sits at a table. Gina is sweeping up the floor. Cole sits at the bar. Duncan stands behind the bar.

DUNCAN. Is this your first time on St. John?

RAYMOND. Our first, yes. Our very first. We've heard talk of the place, of course. We have seen the pictures and read the brochures. But to be here is something else entirely. Something not to be imagined. I mean, look at the purity of that landscape. It's fantastic. Extraordinary.

DUNCAN. So it is.

RAYMOND. The whiteness of that sand. The utter whiteness. And the emerald blue of that water. Really. It quite transcends anything I've ever seen.

GINA. Feeling better?

EMILY. Yes. Thank you.

GINA. Another drink?

EMILY. I ... certainly.

GINA. You, sir?

RAYMOND. Please, call me Raymond.

GINA. All right then, Raymond. One more?

RAYMOND.   I don't mind if I do. *(Duncan mixes the drinks.)* Now, if I may be so bold as to ask, why is it that this establishment of yours is planted so very far off of the main road?

GINA.   A good question.

RAYMOND.   I'm only asking because the man at the hotel said that there was nothing of any special interest on this side of the island.

GINA.   He was right.

RAYMOND.   He told us to avoid it altogether.

DUNCAN.   But you didn't listen to him.

RAYMOND.   Well, obviously not.

DUNCAN.   And why is that?

RAYMOND.   I believe I already said. We were lost.

DUNCAN.   Yes, but some might say not by accident.

RAYMOND.   I don't follow you.

DUNCAN.   Some might say there are two kinds of people in this world. Those who follow the beaten track. And those who fall off of it entirely.

RAYMOND.   I see.

DUNCAN.   And there you have it.

RAYMOND.   Have what?

DUNCAN.   My point.

RAYMOND.   Which is?

DUNCAN.   This island has been turned into a national park. A cruise port. A tropical paradise for the casual tourist. And that's fine, for some people. But for others, well, they might be looking for something different. Something not to be found in the almighty guide book. It's for those people, those others, that I built this bar. *(Pause.)* At least, that was the original intent.

RAYMOND.   Here, here. I like your attitude, sir. I like it very much. *(Gina serves them their drinks.)* Again, to your health.

DUNCAN.   And yours.

COLE.   And ours. To our health. To all of our health. *(They drink. A moment.)*

RAYMOND.   I would dearly love to get out on that water.

DUNCAN.   Oh, yes?

RAYMOND.   Yes. To sail it. To see the island from out there on a day such as this.

COLE.   Well, you still can.

RAYMOND.   And how is that?

COLE.   I can take you.

RAYMOND.   You?

COLE.   Don't look so surprised. I still have my bearings. And my boat.

RAYMOND.   Where?

COLE.   There. Down on the beach. See it?

RAYMOND.   Oh, yes. And, uh ... are you a licensed tour guide, Mr. — ?

COLE.   Cole. I am happy to say that I am not. But I have something that no ordinary guide could hope to offer you.

RAYMOND.   And what is that?

COLE.   You came all this way for the local color, no?

RAYMOND.   Well, yes.

COLE.   Well, then — *(He stands up.)* I am that local color.

RAYMOND.   I appreciate the offer, but, no, I couldn't possibly leave my wife.

EMILY.   No, no, darling, you go. I'll be fine. I'll just sit here quietly.

RAYMOND.   But, my dear, that spill you took —

EMILY.   I'm all right now. Really.

RAYMOND.   Are you sure?

EMILY.   I'm sure.

RAYMOND.   But are you quite certain?

EMILY.   Raymond, please, go and enjoy the day.

RAYMOND.   Well, I suppose, I — *(Pause.)* All right then, why not?

COLE.   Good. What are you drinking?

RAYMOND.   Scotch.

COLE.   Duncan, a bottle of your best Scotch for our heyday

in the sun. *(Duncan tosses him a bottle.)*

RAYMOND.   And how much for the tour, Mr. ... Cole?

COLE.   No, no, no. If you have a nice time, you buy me a drink. If not, Duncan here will buy you one.

RAYMOND.   Well, all right. *(He finishes his drink. A moment.)* I must say, I am transported. To have been standing in the midst of Manhattan traffic only this morning. And now to be here. In this paradise. It is all slightly unreal.

COLE.   Are you done talking?

RAYMOND.   I am.

COLE.   Then let's go. *(He and Raymond exit.)*

EMILY.   Will they be gone long?

DUNCAN.   As long as that bottle lasts.

GINA.   With Cole's thirst that'll be about twenty minutes.

DUNCAN.   Or less.

GINA.   Yes, probably less. *(Pause.)* You sure you're feeling better?

EMILY.   Yes, I am. I really am. I don't know what came over me.

GINA.   The heat.

EMILY.   Yes, quite possibly that.

GINA.   It does burn some days. Burns me right through. But you get used to it.

EMILY.   You're not from here originally?

GINA.   No, I came down on vacation. Like you. But I never went back.

EMILY.   Why not?

GINA.   Well. *(She laughs.)* I was with a man.

EMILY.   Oh?

GINA.   Someone I knew from the old neighborhood. Or thought I knew. This guy was always coming into the restaurant where I worked wearing these fine clothes and flashing a wad of bills. And he made me laugh. Then one day he offered to bring me down here as his guest on an all-expense-paid cruise. Seven nights in paradise. No strings attached. Well, I hadn't ever seen anything but the South Side of Chicago and I thought I could handle him. But when we got to the hotel I found out differently.

EMILY. What happened?

GINA. He said, "Honey, I brought you all the way here, but if you want to go back, you're going to have to give me something."

EMILY. Oh.

GINA. Well, I wasn't about to give him anything but a slap in the face. So he sailed away. And I stayed behind.

EMILY. What did you do?

GINA. I got a job waiting tables in town. And I met someone there. A local man. We fell in love. One thing led to another. *(Pause.)* And I never left. *(Pause.)* I mean, I still think about it sometimes, but then I think where? Where would I go? Where would my life really be any different than it is right here? *(Pause.)* You know what I'm saying?

EMILY. I ... think so.

GINA. Well. *(She goes to the door and looks out.)* It's a slow day.

DUNCAN. Yes.

GINA. Slow and easy with no more customers in sight. *(Pause.)* I guess I'll be heading out. *(Pause.)* If that's all right with you.

DUNCAN. Yes, fine.

GINA. Fine. *(She goes to the door. She turns and looks at him. A moment.)* One way or the other. *(She exits. Silence.)*

DUNCAN. Another drink?

EMILY. No, I'm all right. Thank you. *(Pause.)*

DUNCAN. Where are you from?

EMILY. New York. Manhattan.

DUNCAN. Whereabouts in Manhattan?

EMILY. The Upper East Side.

DUNCAN. Well, then this is something of a busman's holiday for you.

EMILY. How do you mean?

DUNCAN. I mean you've come all the way from the east side

of one island to spend your money on the east side of another.

EMILY.   There is hardly a comparison.

DUNCAN.   No, I'm sure of it. *(Pause.)*

EMILY.   Have you ever been?

DUNCAN.   Where?

EMILY.   To Manhattan.

DUNCAN.   No.

EMILY.   No?

DUNCAN.   No, ma'am. Not in this lifetime. Not that I can recall. *(Pause.)*

EMILY.   How long have you lived here?

DUNCAN.   A time. A few years. More years than I would care to admit. *(Pause.)*

EMILY.   Where are you from?

DUNCAN.   California.

EMILY.   Oh?

DUNCAN.   Southern California.

EMILY.   Where?

DUNCAN.   A small town. A desert town. You would never have heard of it.

EMILY.   You could try me.

DUNCAN.   No.

EMILY.   I know that area quite well.

DUNCAN.   Believe me, the name wouldn't mean anything to you. *(Pause.)*

EMILY.   So what brought you to the islands?

DUNCAN.   A boat. *(Pause.)* A job. I'd been promised a place tending bar at a hotel on St. Thomas. But when I got there I found out that the position had been filled. So I started up my own business. My own bar. This one here that you're sitting in. That your husband has abandoned you to. *(Pause.)* And that pretty much brings us up to date. *(Pause.)*

EMILY.   Your name is Duncan.

DUNCAN.   Yes.

EMILY.   Duncan what?

DUNCAN. Crawford.

EMILY. Crawford?

DUNCAN. Yes.

EMILY. That's an interesting name.

DUNCAN. Oh?

EMILY. Don't you think so?

DUNCAN. Well, to tell you the truth, I hadn't given the matter much thought.

EMILY. No, I can see how that would be. It being your name and all. *(Pause.)* My name is Emily.

DUNCAN. Oh, yes?

EMILY. Emily Miles.

DUNCAN. How do you do, Emily Miles?

EMILY. Oh, better now than an hour ago. And better an hour ago than I have been for several months. And before that for several years. *(Pause.)* It hasn't always been Emily Miles.

DUNCAN. No?

EMILY. No. Before I was married, before I married my husband, it was something else. Another name. My maiden name.

DUNCAN. Well, that's the way it usually works.

EMILY. It was Brown.

DUNCAN. Brown?

EMILY. Yes. A common name. A name that speaks of common things. The earth. The changing seasons. The bottom of one's shoe. *(Pause.)*

I met a man once. His name was Black. We had a good laugh about that, this man and I. Two shades of nature meeting accidentally. Two strangers on the color wheel. Well, I was on the color wheel. He was slightly off. But then he was always slightly off. I think that's why I liked him. And when we stopped laughing, this man and I, we found ourselves looking at each other for the longest time. And then I fell. I simply fell into his arms. *(Pause.)*

I was very young at the time. Very impressionable. And when he asked me to marry him, this man named Black, I said

SCENE THREE

Early afternoon. The following day. Raymond sits at the bar. Duncan stands behind it.

RAYMOND. I do find that when one is on holiday it is almost essential to locate a room, a place, a situation where one can feel totally relaxed. Where one can sit and reflect and see the ground underneath one's feet. There is only so much running about that a body can take. After a time, the changing landscapes all begin to blur together. One town, one city, one countryside becomes indistinguishable from the next. I suppose that the calm and sanctity of a hotel room might provide some people with a temporary sense of relief, but I myself find the damned things to be unbearably depressing. I had much rather be out and about and in the midst of my surroundings. That is the way to travel. The way to absorb a culture. To sit absolutely still and allow the society to carry on around you as if you yourself were not really there. *(Silence.)* My wife is not a well woman.
DUNCAN. Oh?
RAYMOND. No. *(Pause.)* You may have surmised this from the manner in which she spoke to you yesterday after I departed. From the tale that she told. She informed me last night that she had related to you the story of her life. No?
DUNCAN. Yes. She — *(Pause.)* Mentioned ... something.
RAYMOND. Something. The man is a master of understatement. The man is courtesy personified. *(Pause.)*

I first met Emily some years ago at a dinner party hosted by a mutual acquaintance. I was drawn to her immediately. This strange and fascinating woman. Like an oil painting come to life. A creature from a dream. I could see that she was immersed in sadness. Encased in sorrow. And I could not turn away from her. *(Pause.)*

31

At first, she would have nothing to do with me. Oh, she thought I was interesting enough. And amusing. But she was used to living alone. Being alone. She had a large apartment filled with dust and dark corridors and empty rooms. A most disturbing place. I would go there in the evenings and we would sit. Sometimes we'd take a walk and stop in somewhere for a drink. A meal. A midnight conversation. And, in time, she began to think of me as a friend. A confidant. Someone who would always be present for her. Who would remain wholly committed to the idea of drawing her out of herself and into the world. *(Pause.)*

Eventually we were married and I asked her to live with me, but she said no. If we are to live together, she insisted, then it was to be in her home. Her apartment. And, because I wanted her and wanted to be with her, I did as she asked. I moved into that place that smelt of melancholy. And old memories. And for the first few months I thought that I began to detect a change in her. Some small measure of happiness that had actually crept into her being. I realize now, of course, that it was a lie. An illusion she created to please me. She was still the same withdrawn woman that I had fallen in love with. And the cause of her grief was unknown to me. It was something that she simply refused to discuss.

DUNCAN.   She was obsessed.

RAYMOND.   Yes.

DUNCAN.   With this man.

RAYMOND.   Indeed.

DUNCAN.   This ... Crawford Black.

RAYMOND.   He had left her at the altar at the tender age of nineteen and she had never recovered from it. And that is why we were there. In her apartment. And why we are there still. To this day.

DUNCAN.   Because it's the last place that she'd been with him.

RAYMOND.   Yes.

DUNCAN.   How did you find out about all this?

RAYMOND.   A man came to the door one day. A private investigator. She had hired him, you see, to find her friend. Her former fiancé. He didn't know that I knew nothing about it and so handed me his full report. I read the thing. Astonished. Incredulous that she had been so abused. That she could not forget. And that she had gone to such great lengths to locate this man. *(Pause.)*

I confronted her with my knowledge and she told me everything. The entire tale. It was almost as if she was glad that I had stumbled onto her secret and uncovered the truth. *(Pause.)*

This did not stop her, of course. She continued to hunt for the man who haunted her still. Calls would come at odd hours. Information would arrive. And all of it was centered on this man. And now, of course, now after years of searching, she believes that she has found him. And she believes him to be you.

DUNCAN.   But why?

RAYMOND.   She has recently discovered that he left the country some years ago. That he first came to St. Thomas. And then St. John.

DUNCAN.   Do we look anything alike?

RAYMOND.   I've seen the photographs. There is a dim resemblance. That is all.

DUNCAN.   And our names.

RAYMOND.   Yes. The coincidence of the names. There is that. *(Pause.)* I didn't know, of course, that this was why we were coming here. I was under the assumption that we were simply taking a holiday. I was so happy to be going away with her. Ecstatic to be getting her out of that city. I can't tell you. But then last night she told me everything. I have been tricked, you see. Deceived. We are not here on a vacation. We are here on a vendetta. *(Pause.)*

DUNCAN.   I have to ask you this.

RAYMOND. Go on.

DUNCAN. Has your wife — ?

RAYMOND. What?

DUNCAN. Seen anyone?

RAYMOND. As in a doctor? A therapist? A professional counselor?

DUNCAN. Yes.

RAYMOND. She's seen them all. All of them. And all are equally baffled.

DUNCAN. What do they say?

RAYMOND. That nothing will satisfy her until she finds the man. Until she speaks with him. Until she discovers why it is that he left her. *(Pause.)* I have a proposition for you.

DUNCAN. Oh?

RAYMOND. I wish to hire you to impersonate this man. *(Pause.)*

DUNCAN. You — ?

RAYMOND. I want you to pretend to be him. For a night. That is all.

DUNCAN. Why?

RAYMOND. To offer her the possibility of reconciliation. A chance to confront her past. To come face to face with the man who abandoned her. To forgive him. To forget him.

DUNCAN. How do I know she won't come after me with knife? *(Raymond laughs.)*

RAYMOND. I don't think that's in her plans.

DUNCAN. And you want to pay me for this?

RAYMOND. Yes.

DUNCAN. You're crazy.

RAYMOND. I am. Yes. With jealousy. Of her former life that I can have no access to. Of a shadow on the wall that will not go away. *(Pause.)*

DUNCAN. How much?

RAYMOND. Ten thousand dollars.

DUNCAN. Ten ... thousand — ?

34

RAYMOND.   American dollars. I believe they're still welcome. In some parts of the world.

DUNCAN.   Christ.

RAYMOND.   It is a tidy sum, I think. For a single night's work.

DUNCAN.   No, no, I mean, yes, it's generous, but —

RAYMOND.   But what?

DUNCAN.   I can't do it.

RAYMOND.   Why not?

DUNCAN.   I don't know the man. What he'd say. How he'd behave.

RAYMOND.   That doesn't matter.

DUNCAN.   His background. His history.

RAYMOND.   No, it makes no difference, don't you see? She already believes that he's you. That you are him. That part of it is taken care of. There will be no need to convince her. She has already done that for us.

DUNCAN.   No, look, I really don't —

RAYMOND.   I can tell you the facts. The necessary essentials. Everything that I have learned about this man.

DUNCAN.   But —

RAYMOND.   All that remains is for you to fill in the blank spaces.

DUNCAN.   She won't believe me.

RAYMOND.   She *will* believe you. She *wants* to believe you. *(Pause.)* You would be doing us both a great favor. And you would be well paid for your efforts. *(Pause.)*

DUNCAN.   What do you do?

RAYMOND.   Pardon me?

DUNCAN.   For a living? Where do you get that kind of money?

RAYMOND.   I — *(Pause.)* Am a banker.

DUNCAN.   A banker?

RAYMOND.   An investment banker. I ... help people to invest their earnings. Their capital.

DUNCAN.   You talk them into things.

35

RAYMOND. Well —

DUNCAN. Things they might not want.

RAYMOND. Now look —

DUNCAN. Or need.

RAYMOND. That is unfair. *(Pause.)* I am offering a straight forward business proposition. There is no hidden agenda here. No secret purpose other than what I have stated. I see the possibility of rescuing my marriage. And I am prepared to pay for it.

DUNCAN. Ten thousand dollars.

RAYMOND. Yes.

DUNCAN. When?

RAYMOND. What?

DUNCAN. When would you want me to do this thing?

RAYMOND. Tonight. She's coming to see you tonight. Tomorrow we fly back to the States. *(Pause.)* Please. *(Pause.)* Will you help me?

SCENE FOUR

Evening. Duncan is cleaning up. Gina sits at a table drinking with Cole.

GINA. No, the boy was only eight months old when his father and I split up, so the child's got no memory of him. No sense of who he was. Which, so far as I'm concerned, is a blessing as the man was a con artist and a thief.

COLE. A thief?

GINA. He used to steal things.

COLE. What things?

GINA. I never told you?

COLE. No.

GINA. Passports. Money. Loose change from the pockets of tourists. He'd hide out in the brush on the beaches at night and when people went for a swim he'd steal them blind. I

36

didn't know that, of course, when he and I started up, but when I found out I told him that it was no good. That it had to stop. Well, that man wasn't about to let anyone tell him what to. Especially a woman. He grabbed hold of me and threw me up against the wall and told me to stay out of his business or he'd kill me. Then he laughed and kissed me instead. I sank down onto my knees. Scared half out of my mind. And I let him make love to me. But all the time I was making other plans. *(Pause.)*

COLE.   Whatever happened to him?

GINA.   He left me.

COLE.   Oh?

GINA.   Eventually.

COLE.   When?

GINA.   Right after I hit him in the head. *(Pause.)*

COLE.   You — ?

GINA.   Hit him in the head. With a bat. While he was asleep. *(She laughs.)*

COLE.   What did he do?

GINA.   He woke up. *(She laughs again.)* He was bleeding and he came after me and I told him if he hurt me, if he threatened me, if he so much as came near me or my child, ever, ever again, I would go to the authorities and I would not stop talking. *(Pause.)* So he left.

COLE.   And how was he a con artist?

GINA.   Well, he tricked me into falling in love with him, didn't he? *(Pause.)* So my child never knew the man which is good. But Duncan, here, he looks up to. Duncan, he emulates.

DUNCAN.   Gina —

GINA.   Yes?

DUNCAN.   You need to talk to the boy.

GINA.   Oh, believe me, I already have. *(Pause.)* I told him that it's okay to like you. To even look up to you. But that under no circumstances should he be thinking of you as a father. Or family. Or a man to be counted on because when it comes right

37

down to it we could both wake up tomorrow and you could be on a boat. At sea. With strangers.

DUNCAN. No.

GINA. What?

DUNCAN. That's not going to happen.

GINA. Why not?

DUNCAN. Because the people I told you about set sail today. *(Pause.)* It's too late. *(Pause.)* I'm here.

GINA. So where does that leave us?

DUNCAN. I.... *(Pause.)* Don't know. *(A moment. Then Emily enters. Duncan sees her.)* Hello.

EMILY. Hello.

GINA. Oh. *(She turns and sees Emily.)* Well, you look like you're feeling better.

EMILY. Yes, I am.

GINA. That's good. *(She stands up.)* Can I get you something to drink?

DUNCAN. I'll ... get her something.

GINA. Oh?

DUNCAN. Yes. *(To Emily.)* What would you like?

EMILY. Am I ... interrupting?

DUNCAN. No.

GINA. No, absolutely not. This is a public room. And I, for one, am on my way home.

COLE. I'll walk with you.

DUNCAN. Gina —

GINA. Yes? *(Duncan reaches behind the bar and produces a package. He goes to Gina. He holds it out for her.)* What's this?

DUNCAN. A gift. For the boy. For his birthday. *(Pause.)* It's not much. It's only a box. A wooden box with some carvings. I saw it at the market in town and I thought, well, maybe he could use it for something. Like those shells of his. Or those coins he likes to collect. *(Pause.)* I thought he might like it. *(Gina stares at the box.)*

GINA. Well, that's thoughtful of you.

38

DUNCAN. No —

GINA. No, it is. But I don't think it's a good idea for you to be giving him any gifts right now. Do you? *(Pause.)* I'll see you tomorrow. *(She exits. Duncan puts the package down. Cole goes to the door. He turns to them. A moment.)*

COLE. I was going to say something, but now I can't remember what. My mind. It is starting to go. I forget what I was going to do. I walk into a room and don't know why I'm there. Everything falls out of my head. All but that one day. The last one with my wife. That I can remember like it was this morning. Funny. *(Pause.)* Oh, well. Maybe tomorrow things will be different, hmm? Maybe tomorrow the fish will jump right up into my boat. Into my hands. Now that would be something. *(Pause.)* Good night. *(He exits. Silence. Duncan looks at Emily.)*

DUNCAN. Martini?

EMILY. No. Something else. A bottle of wine, I think.

DUNCAN. Oh?

EMILY. Will you share it with me?

DUNCAN. I never drink while I'm working.

EMILY. Then stop working.

DUNCAN. Well, I would, but — *(Pause.)* All right. *(He goes behind the bar, replaces the package, and looks for a bottle.)* Red?

EMILY. White.

DUNCAN. Sweet?

EMILY. Dry. *(He finds something and pulls it out. He opens it. He moves to a table and pours two glasses. He raises his glass. She does the same.)*

DUNCAN. Cheers. *(But he doesn't touch his glass to hers. Instead he moves away. He drinks.)*

EMILY. Yes, cheers. *(Then she drinks. A moment.)* She has a boy?

DUNCAN. Who?

EMILY. Your ... friend?

DUNCAN. Yes.

EMILY. How old?

DUNCAN. Seven.

EMILY. What's he like?

DUNCAN. He's ... bright. Curious. Inquisitive.

EMILY. And she? *(Pause.)* What's she like?

DUNCAN. Gina.

EMILY. Yes.

DUNCAN. Hard. Opinionated. *(Pause.)* Loving.

EMILY. Well, I do hope you are better to her than you were to me.

DUNCAN. Look —

EMILY. Yes?

DUNCAN. I know what you think.

EMILY. Really?

DUNCAN. You think that I'm this man.

EMILY. I do.

DUNCAN. This ... Crawford Black.

EMILY. Correct.

DUNCAN. But I'm not.

EMILY. You say that you're not, but I know that you are.

DUNCAN. How do you know?

EMILY. I know. I simply ... know. *(Pause.)* My husband came to see you today.

DUNCAN. Oh, yes?

EMILY. Yes. *(Pause.)*

DUNCAN. What makes you say that?

EMILY. Well, he told me that he was going to sit out by the pool this morning, but when I went looking for him the man at the desk said he'd left the hotel sometime ago in the rental car. *(Pause.)* Where else would he go? *(Pause.)*

DUNCAN. I —

EMILY. Please don't deny it. It will only be embarrassing for both of us. *(Pause.)* What did he want? *(Pause.)*

DUNCAN. A drink.

EMILY. What else? *(Pause.)*

DUNCAN. He wanted me to pretend to be this man.

EMILY. Ah. *(Pause.)* But why would he want you to do that? I mean, that's who you are. Why pretend otherwise?

DUNCAN. Because he doesn't happen to think that I'm him.

EMILY. And what do you think?

DUNCAN. Seriously?

EMILY. Yes.

DUNCAN. I think you're both crazy. Insane. Twisted. Deranged. And possibly dangerous.

EMILY. Well, you've got that right. *(Pause.)* And what did you say to him?

DUNCAN. I said, no. I'm not interested in trying to pretend to be anyone but myself. I have a hard enough time with that. I don't want to impersonate another man. Not for any amount of money.

EMILY. He offered to pay you?

DUNCAN. Yes.

EMILY. How much? *(Pause.)* I'm curious to learn how much my peace of mind means to my darling Raymond. *(Pause.)*

DUNCAN. Ten thousand.

EMILY. I see. *(Pause.)*

DUNCAN. Are you disappointed?

EMILY. No, I think it's quite generous, don't you?

DUNCAN. I do.

EMILY. But you said, no.

DUNCAN. I did.

EMILY. I'm so glad.

DUNCAN. Why?

EMILY. Because it would have been such a waste of money.

DUNCAN. Oh?

EMILY. I already know that it's you. I'm convinced now. Unequivocally and without a doubt. *(Pause.)*

I *was* in doubt when I first walked in here yesterday. When I set foot in your saloon uncertain of what I might find after all these years. But then I heard your voice. And saw your face. And looked into your eyes. Which do not change. Which cannot be altered. And I knew who you were. Without question. I knew. *(Pause.)*

I don't know how you did it, Crawford. I really don't. You disappeared without a trace. Without so much as a single clue. No withdrawals of money. Or credit card charges. Or travel reservations. No airline tickets. No passport. No luggage. Nothing. It was as if you had simply ceased to be. *(Pause.)*

The detectives I hired, the private investigators, were most expert in their lines of inquiry. No one knew a thing. Your family. Your friends and associates. The police. Not even the federal government. Yes, I went so far as to have you listed as a missing person. Had your photograph distributed and a description put on file. Still there were no leads. Not for the longest time. *(Pause.)*

Then one day. Something. A telephone call in the middle of the night. A man had spotted you, or someone who looked like you, in a seafood restaurant on the island of St. Thomas. This man was down here on vacation with his family. He had worked for one of the investigators I hired some years ago. And he remembered you. Your story. It haunted him, he said. The way a man could be there one minute and not the next. And he remembered your face. Your features. So he called me from a pay phone in the parking lot. I told him to follow you. He said that he would. But when he went back into the restaurant you were gone. *(Pause.)*

He asked a few questions. And it turned out that one of the waitresses knew you. She said you owned a bar out on St. John. Said your name was Crawford. Duncan Crawford. *(Pause.)*

It's all right. You can tell me. You can confess the truth. I'm not out for blood. I only want to know.

DUNCAN. What do you want to know?

EMILY. Why it is that you left me. *(A moment. Then Duncan goes to the door. He looks out.)*

DUNCAN. The water's choppy tonight. Some people I know are sailing on it. It'll be slow for them. Slow going. And to-morrow, they say, it's going to rain. *(Pause.)* Yes.

EMILY.   What?

DUNCAN.   Yes, it's me. I am the man. My name is Crawford Black. *(A moment.)* More wine?

EMILY.   Oh, yes. Absolutely. Yes. *(He moves to the table and fills her glass. He fills his own. He drinks.)*

DUNCAN.   Where do you want me to start?

EMILY.   Tell me about that night.

DUNCAN.   What night?

EMILY.   The last night in my apartment.

DUNCAN.   When we made love.

EMILY.   And you got up off the floor.

DUNCAN.   And I said I was going out for a pack of cigarettes.

EMILY.   And you left.

DUNCAN.   And never came back.

EMILY.   No, never. *(Pause.)* Tell me about that.

DUNCAN.   Well. *(Pause.)* I started walking. To my own apartment. Like I usually did. And thinking. All the time thinking. Tomorrow I'll be married. Tomorrow I'll be wed. And I could see it. My life. As I knew it was then. And knew it would be. And then something happened. My imagination began to wander. And I asked myself now what would it be like if I really was never to return? Not only to you, but to my existence here as I know it to be? And know it will be? Where would I start? What would I do? And the idea made me laugh as I wasn't so much thinking about myself in the specific as a man in general. Well, I thought. First, that man would have to keep walking. Past his residence. Out of his traditional way. And then beyond. And for some odd reason, to amuse myself, I guess, I found myself doing that very thing. I walked right past my building and continued on. Only for a short ways, I thought, only for a block or two. And then it was three. Then four. Then I was several miles off my regular path standing in the center of town outside the bus station —

EMILY.   Port Authority.

DUNCAN.   Yes. Port Authority. And then I was inside the station buying a ticket and then I was on a bus and then the bus was in motion and I watched the building, the block, the entire island disappear, and I saw everything that I knew, everything that I was certain of, disappear with it. *(Pause.)*

At this point, I will tell you, I had no idea what I was doing. No real concept at all. It was all in my head. It was an exercise. A game. I thought I'd get off the bus at some point and call a car and go back to Manhattan. But I didn't. I stayed on that bus. And I watched the lights on the highway. And the towns going by. And the row after row of houses that all looked the same. And I thought about the people inside those houses. Dreaming of all the places they'd never see and all the possibilities they'd never pursue. And then it was morning and I was getting off the bus somewhere in the middle of Pennsylvania in a place I'd never heard of looking at people I'd never seen before and I felt.... *(Pause.)*

Somehow uniquely alive. *(Pause.)*

I went into a diner and ordered a cup of coffee and then a refill. And I watched as the clock on the wall made its rounds. And I knew you'd be getting up and showering and putting on that white dress. And that you'd go to that church and our friends, our families, would arrive and take their seats and before I knew it, before I could move to correct the action I'd taken, the ceremony was over and I was not married. I was sitting in a diner in Pennsylvania and asking for my check. *(Pause.)*

I panicked then. Didn't know what to do. I wanted to go back. I really did. Wanted it so badly. I can't tell you. But I knew it was too late. That I had stepped over some sort of a line into another reality. Now it was as if I was coming out of a dream. Now I was looking at my reflection in the bathroom mirror and running cold water over my face and asking myself who that ghost of a man was. *(Pause.)*

I counted the money in my pocket. There wasn't much, but it was enough to get me on another bus. I traveled to the

Midwest. To some industrial town on the edge of Indiana. I kicked around for a few days, spent the remainder of my resources gambling, and finally got a job at a filling station. I earned enough cash to buy some false identification and a used car. And I got in that car and drove across the country. *(Pause.)*

I lived in Seattle for a while. Then Portland. Then down the coast to San Francisco. And then Los Angeles. And then finally San Diego. I never stayed in the cities themselves, but somewhere outside. Some small town where I mostly kept to myself. I held down a series of occupations that I could never have imagined myself performing in my former life. I was a house painter for a while. And then a lawn boy. And then I carted away other people's garbage. I was thinking about going down south into Mexico, but I didn't have a passport and couldn't afford a fake one. Then I met a man playing pool one night who was sailing down into the Virgin Islands and needed a second mate. I convinced him that I had the experience though, in fact, I had none, but once we were at sea it was too late. The poor guy was stuck with me. I did the best I could and learned along the way and finally we docked in St. Thomas and that's where I got out. And I told the first person I met that my name was Duncan. Duncan Crawford. *(Pause.)*

That was seventeen years ago.

EMILY. Yes. *(Pause.)* Do you remember the first time we met?

DUNCAN. And exchanged names. Black for brown. Brown for black. Yes, I remember that. *(Pause.)* It was in the museum.

EMILY. The Met.

DUNCAN. Yes, the Metropolitan Museum.

EMILY. We were both looking at the same painting.

DUNCAN. We were staring at the same one.

EMILY. You were standing next to me. And the silence was unbearable. And then finally you spoke.

DUNCAN. I said something.

EMILY. Do you remember what it was that you said?

DUNCAN. I said.... *(Pause.)* Hello.

EMILY. You said that the painting moved you in a strange and unfamiliar way.

DUNCAN. I did?

EMILY. Yes.

DUNCAN. I actually said that?

EMILY. Yes. And I knew you didn't mean it, but I didn't mind because it got us talking. And then we walked out of the museum and into traffic. And it started to rain. And we shared a cab. *(Pause.)* And you kissed me.

DUNCAN. Yes.

EMILY. There in the back seat with a stranger watching us in the mirror.

DUNCAN. Yes.

EMILY. You kissed me and I started to shake and you asked me what was wrong. And do you remember what I said?

DUNCAN. You said.... *(Pause.)* You were scared.

EMILY. I said I was frightened of falling into the arms of a man who I had met only moments ago. Frightened. And exhilarated. And because I was unsure, because I was of two minds, you asked the cab to stop. And you got out. And you said good-bye.

DUNCAN. Yes.

EMILY. You behaved like a gentleman.

DUNCAN. Yes, I did. And do you know what?

EMILY. What?

DUNCAN. I cursed myself for it all the way home. *(Pause.)*

EMILY. Later you found my name in the telephone directory, my phone number, my address, and you called me and we met and went for a drive in the country and you pulled the car over to the side of the road and you had me. There in the front seat of that car. You simply had me.

DUNCAN. Yes.

EMILY. Your hands were all over me. There was nothing I could do. Nothing I wanted to do. I wanted you. There. Inside me. Your face in my hands. Your mouth on my body. Your teeth on my skin. *(Pause.)* Do you recall what you said afterwards?

DUNCAN. I — *(Pause.)* No. I don't recall what I said. I only recall what I did.

EMILY. You said that I moved you in a strange and unfamiliar way.

DUNCAN. Oh, God.

EMILY. It was comical. I laughed. But this time I could tell something else.

DUNCAN. What was that?

EMILY. This time I could tell that you actually meant it. *(Pause.)* We were inseparable after that. Literally. On the floor. Or the stairwell. Once in an elevator.

DUNCAN. I remember that.

EMILY. Between floors.

DUNCAN. I remember that building.

EMILY. Between places.

DUNCAN. I wonder —

EMILY. What?

DUNCAN. Did we ever — ?

EMILY. Yes?

DUNCAN. Make love in a bed?

EMILY. I don't think so.

DUNCAN. No. *(Pause.)*

EMILY. I think there are moments in this life that change us beyond recognition. That open us up to the hard edges and the rough elements. And afterwards we are never the same. We are transformed into other people. And you were that to me. *(Pause.)* You were that to me. *(Pause.)* And then when you went away, when you fell off the face of this earth so suddenly, and left me behind to decipher the riddle, it was as if I had fallen, too. As if I had disappeared. And when I found myself again I discovered that you were not gone. You were still there. Inside me. *(A moment.)*

DUNCAN. I have something to say.

EMILY.   Yes?

DUNCAN.   Something that I've been meaning to tell you.

EMILY.   Go on.

DUNCAN.   I always felt that a part of me did go to the church that day. And did marry you. And remains married to you still. *(Pause.)* And that's the truth. *(Pause.)*

EMILY.   Why did you leave me, Crawford?

DUNCAN.   I told you —

EMILY.   No. What put that thought in your head? Where did that feeling come from?

DUNCAN.   I don't know.

EMILY.   Something I said? Something I didn't say?

DUNCAN.   No.

EMILY.   Something I didn't do?

DUNCAN.   It wasn't that.

EMILY.   Then what?

DUNCAN.   I was frightened.

EMILY.   Of me?

DUNCAN.   Of myself. *(Pause.)* I was so in love with you, so blind to anything but you, that I was afraid if I stayed there, if I married you, if I gave myself over to you, I would completely disappear. I would lose myself inside you. And I would never discover who I was. *(Pause.)* That's all, Emily. It was never anything to do with you. It was me. My inability to give myself to you. The way I wanted to. The way I knew I should. *(Pause.)*

EMILY.   You said my name.

DUNCAN.   What?

EMILY.   My name. You said it exactly the way you used to say it. *(Pause.)* Say it again. *(Pause.)*

DUNCAN.   Emily.

EMILY.   Again.

DUNCAN.   Emily.

EMILY.   Again.

DUNCAN.   Emily. *(Pause.)* Forgive me. *(A moment. Then she moves to him. She touches his hands. His face. They kiss. The kiss*

turns into a full embrace. He pulls her into him. They continue. Then
suddenly she pulls away. She goes to the door and looks out. She makes
a decision. She turns and looks back at him. And she walks out onto
the deck and down onto the beach. A moment. Then he follows her.)

SCENE FIVE

Early afternoon. The following day. Raymond stands in the
doorway looking at Duncan who stands behind the bar.

DUNCAN.   She knew that you'd been here. In the afternoon.
Knew that we'd talked. She wanted to know what about. So I
told her. I said that you'd wanted me to go along with her story.
To pretend to be this man. That you'd offered payment. I told
her that I'd said no. That I had refused. We opened a bottle.
We began to talk. One thing led to another. *(Pause.)* And I con-
fessed. *(Pause.)* I told her who I was. *(Pause.)* I said that I was
the man. *(Pause.)*
RAYMOND.   Brilliant.
DUNCAN.   Oh —
RAYMOND.   No, really. Absolutely brilliant. To turn the lie in-
side itself that way.
DUNCAN.   Well —
RAYMOND.   It was a coup. A masterstroke.
DUNCAN.   I don't know about that.
RAYMOND.   I do. *(Pause.)* She came back to the hotel this
morning around four A.M. I heard her slip into bed and pre-
tended to be asleep. Then, at breakfast, she told me every-
thing.
DUNCAN.   Everything?
RAYMOND.   Oh, yes. Exactly as you have described. And I will
tell you this. She is changed woman.
DUNCAN.   Really?
RAYMOND.   Transformed.

DUNCAN. Well, I'm … happy for you.

RAYMOND. She honestly believes that she has finally found the man who hurt her so deeply those many years ago. She has found him. And she is ready to forget. *(Pause.)* I can hardly thank you enough.

DUNCAN. Raymond —

RAYMOND. Yes?

DUNCAN. There's something that … happened between us.

RAYMOND. Really?

DUNCAN. Something that you need to know.

RAYMOND. No. *(Pause.)* No, there is nothing else that I need to know. *(A moment. Then Raymond goes to a table. He pulls out his checkbook.)* I believe the amount we agreed upon was ten thousand dollars. *(Pause.)*

DUNCAN. Yes.

RAYMOND. Do you happen to have a pen? *(Duncan finds a pen behind the bar and brings it to him. Raymond begins to write out the check.)* I heard they thought it might rain today.

DUNCAN. Yes, that was the rumor.

RAYMOND. Instead it's absolutely clear. Clear and perfect. A perfect day for returning home. *(He rips out the check and holds it out for Duncan.)* Here we are. *(Duncan does not move. He only looks at the check.)* Go ahead. You've earned it.

DUNCAN. Listen —

RAYMOND. What?

DUNCAN. Did you ever — ?

RAYMOND. Yes?

DUNCAN. I mean — *(Pause.)* Did it ever occur to you that I might in fact be the man?

RAYMOND. Who?

DUNCAN. Crawford Black.

RAYMOND. Oh, him. *(He laughs.)* Never.

DUNCAN. Really?

RAYMOND. Not for a moment. Because if you were, if you really were the man who had caused my Emily such unmitigated

50

grief, then I would have to do something about it, wouldn't I? Then I would have to kill you. *(He smiles.)* Or something.

DUNCAN. Yes.

RAYMOND. Instead I'm giving you my money. *(Pause.)* Take it. *(A moment. Then Duncan reaches for the check and puts it in his pocket. Emily enters. He looks up. He sees her.)*

DUNCAN. Hello. *(Raymond turns. He sees her. She looks at the two men.)*

RAYMOND. Hello, my love.

EMILY. I.... *(Pause.)* I came by to tell you that the ferry is leaving a half hour early.

RAYMOND. Oh?

EMILY. A half hour sooner than expected.

RAYMOND. I see.

EMILY. So we have to pack.

RAYMOND. Yes.

EMILY. We have to go.

RAYMOND. Of course.

EMILY. Otherwise we might miss it. *(Pause.)* Our flight, I mean. *(Pause.)*

RAYMOND. I was just saying farewell to our friend.

EMILY. Yes, I can see that. *(A moment. Then she approaches Duncan.)* What did my husband give you? *(Pause.)* What did you just now put in your pocket? *(Pause.)* Crawford?

DUNCAN. I —

RAYMOND. Our address, of course. I told him if he were ever to come through Manhattan he should look us up. *(Emily turns to him.)*

EMILY. You gave him our address?

RAYMOND. Yes. I ... hope that was all right. *(Emily turns back to Duncan.)*

EMILY. Is that true?

DUNCAN. Yes.

EMILY. Is that what you put in your pocket?

DUNCAN. Yes.

EMILY. Our address? *(Pause.)*

DUNCAN. I asked for it.

EMILY. But why?

DUNCAN. What?

EMILY. Why would you do that?

DUNCAN. Well.... *(Pause.)* On the off chance that I ever get to New York, I thought it might be nice to ... see you ... again.

EMILY. No, why would you need that address when it is the same one that I have had for the past twenty years? *(Pause.)* I have never lived anywhere else. I have always been there. Since the night you left me. Our last night together. Why would you need to be reminded of that? *(Pause.)* Yes?

DUNCAN. Well, it's been twenty years and I —

EMILY. Can I see it, please? *(Pause.)* Can I see that address? *(A moment. Then Duncan reaches into his pocket. He pulls out the check and hands it to Emily. She looks at it. Nothing. Then she drops the check on the floor. And her hand goes to her heart. Raymond goes to her.)*

RAYMOND. My love —

EMILY. No. Please. I want ... nothing.

RAYMOND. I am so sorry, I —

EMILY. Nothing.

RAYMOND. Emily — *(He reaches out for her and she slaps his hands away.)*

EMILY. Don't. Touch me. *(She turns on Duncan. She looks him in the eyes.)* Who are you?

DUNCAN. I told you —

EMILY. I don't believe you. I don't believe you. I don't believe you. *(She hits him in the chest. Hard. She shouts.)* WHO ARE YOU? *(She backs away from him. Then she turns and runs out of the bar. A moment. Duncan and Raymond are both motionless. Then Raymond speaks.)*

RAYMOND. I have to go to her. *(Pause.)* Go to her and say ... something. *(Pause.)* What should I say?

DUNCAN. I don't know. *(Pause.)* I honestly don't know what

to tell you. *(Pause.)* Tell her the truth.

RAYMOND. The truth.

DUNCAN. Tell her what you know. What you believe.

RAYMOND. And what is that?

DUNCAN. That you'll never leave her. Not for any reason. Or wrong-doing. Or circumstance. Or situation. Not for any problem. Not for any person. Tell her that you'll be together. You will be with her. Tell her that. *(A moment. Then Raymond exits. Duncan is alone. He walks over to the check. He picks it up off the floor. He looks at it. Cole enters. He goes to the bar and sits. Duncan pockets the check.)*

COLE. Well. It has finally happened. The fish have started ridiculing me. They call me names. They bring their families. Their friends. I have gained a reputation out there. I am the idiot fisherman. I tell you I am ready to give it up. *(Pause.)* Maybe I'll become a bartender.

DUNCAN. Cole?

COLE. Yes?

DUNCAN. I want to buy your boat. *(Pause.)*

COLE. Sorry?

DUNCAN. I said I want to buy your boat.

COLE. My boat?

DUNCAN. Yes.

COLE. What for?

DUNCAN. Are you interested in selling it?

COLE. Why do you want a boat?

DUNCAN. Well, some people I met need a second mate. And they've already set sail. So I have to catch up.

COLE. You're going away?

DUNCAN. I am.

COLE. Where?

DUNCAN. I'm not sure.

COLE. How long?

DUNCAN. I don't know. *(Pause.)* How much do you want?

COLE. Well, now, that boat it has sentimental value.

DUNCAN. How much?

COLE. Sentiment that is hard to put a price on.

DUNCAN. Cole —

COLE. How much do I owe you?

DUNCAN. For what?

COLE. This drink. And the drink I had the day before that. And the day before that. And as far back as I can remember. What is the sum total of my tab?

DUNCAN. I stopped counting several years ago.

COLE. So did I. *(He reaches into his pocket and pulls out a set of keys. He looks at them. A moment. Then he throws them to Duncan. Duncan catches them.)* What should I tell her?

DUNCAN. Tell her.... *(Pause.)* It isn't meant to hurt her. It's only that I have to get away. Tell her.... *(Pause.)* Good-bye.

COLE. I'll tell her that you said nothing at all.

DUNCAN. Yes, I suppose that would be best. *(Pause.)* Well.

COLE. Good-bye, Duncan. *(He holds out his hand. Duncan goes to him and shakes it.)*

DUNCAN. Good-bye now. *(A moment. Then Duncan exits. Cole finishes his whiskey, gets up, and goes behind the bar. He finds a fresh bottle. He opens it, returns to his glass, and pours. Gina enters.)*

GINA. Hello, Cole.

COLE. Gina.

GINA. Nothing biting?

COLE. Not today. But I had a piece of luck.

GINA. Oh?

COLE. I sold my boat.

GINA. Really?

COLE. For a drink.

GINA. To who?

COLE. A man.

GINA. Anyone I know?

COLE. Well now, that depends on what you mean. *(Pause.)* How are you?

GINA. Me?

COLE. Yes.

GINA. I'm fine.

COLE. And the boy?

GINA. He's fine, too.

COLE. That's good.

GINA. Why the sudden interest?

COLE. No, no, I'm only asking.

GINA. Well, we're doing all right. *(Pause.)* I mean, I miss him. *(She laughs.)* I do. *(She sits. A moment.)* It didn't really hit me till this morning how much. I was changing the sheets on the bed. And remembering. Him. Lying there with me. The feeling of what it was like between us. When it was right. And words weren't necessary. I mean, whatever happens from here on out I'll be fine. I know how to take care of myself. But still.... *(Pause.)* I do miss him. *(Pause.)* It's funny, isn't it?

COLE. What's that?

GINA. How someone can get inside you without you even knowing it?

COLE. Yes. *(Pause.)*

GINA. So where is he? *(Pause.)* Cole?

COLE. Well now — *(Duncan enters. He stands in the doorway. He stares at Gina. And it is as if he is seeing her for the first time. Silence.)*

DUNCAN. Hello, Gina.

GINA. Where were you? *(A moment. Then he walks up to Cole and returns the keys. He simply places them in his hand. Then he goes to the bar and pulls the check out of his pocket. He looks at it, finds a match, and sets it on fire. He watches it burn.)* Duncan?

DUNCAN. I was down on the beach thinking about a man I recently heard of who lived in New York City. It seems that he went out for a pack of cigarettes one night and he never came home. And I thought how sad for him. That he had to go halfway around the world in search of some grand adventure. Only to discover that he'd always be coming back to himself. *(The check is now gone.)* Listen.... *(Pause.)* Listen, I think we should get married.

55

GINA. What?

DUNCAN. I think we should get married.

GINA. The two of us?

DUNCAN. Yes.

GINA. To each other?

DUNCAN. That's right. *(Pause.)* I want to live with you. And Simon. In a house. A real house. A home. *(Pause.)* What do you say?

GINA. I ... *(Pause.)* I don't know what to say.

DUNCAN. But you'll think about it.

GINA. Yes, I'll ... think about it.

DUNCAN. Good. *(He walks up to her. He takes her face in his hands. And he kisses her. A moment. Then he goes back behind the bar.)*

GINA. What is it? *(Pause.)* What's happened?

DUNCAN. Nothing's happened. *(He finds a bottle, opens it, pours them each a drink.)* A toast.

GINA. To what?

DUNCAN. To sadness. To the end of it. The end of sadness.

COLE. Now that I will drink to. *(They drink. A moment.)* Did I ever tell you the story of how I lost my wife?

DUNCAN. Yes.

COLE. The story of how I came to be a single man?

DUNCAN. You have.

COLE. The man I am today?

DUNCAN. A hundred times.

COLE. Well, then. *(Pause.)* We were on a boat. My boat. And we'd been drinking. And my wife was laughing. At me. At something I'd said. And then — *(A moment. Then he starts laughing.)* Oh, no.

DUNCAN. What?

COLE. Oh, my God. My God. *(He keeps laughing.)*

GINA. Cole?

COLE. I just remembered.

DUNCAN. Remembered what?

COLE.   What I said to her. That day. To make her laugh. *(He continues laughing. Gina looks at Duncan in confusion. Duncan looks at Gina and smiles.)*

END OF PLAY

PROPERTY LIST

Beer glasses
Cocktail glasses
Ashtrays
Beer bottles
Liquor bottles
Playing cards (DUNCAN)
Shot glass (COLE)
Beer bottle (COLE)
Purse (GINA)
Business cards (GINA)
Towels (GINA)
Money (bills) (DUNCAN)
Wallet (RAYMOND)
Business card (RAYMOND)
Purse (EMILY)
Scotch bottles (DUNCAN)
Cocktail glass (DUNCAN)
Ice (DUNCAN)
Vodka bottle (DUNCAN)
Shaker (DUNCAN)
Martini glass (DUNCAN)
Vermouth bottle (DUNCAN)
Strainer (DUNCAN)
Broom (GINA)
Wine glass (GINA)
Package (DUNCAN)
Wine bottle (DUNCAN)
Bottle opener (DUNCAN)
Wine glasses (DUNCAN)
Checkbook (RAYMOND)
Pen (DUNCAN)
Keys (COLE)
Whiskey bottle (COLE)
Matches (DUNCAN)
Rum bottle (DUNCAN)
Rum glasses (DUNCAN)

COSTUME PLOT

Scene One

COLE
   T-shirt
   Pants
DUNCAN
   Work shirt
   Pants
GINA
   Blouse
   Dress
RAYMOND
   Suit
   Shirt
   Tie
EMILY
   Summer dress

Scene Two

DUNCAN
   Work shirt (same as Scene One)
   Pants (same as Scene One)
RAYMOND
   Suit (same as Scene One)
   Shirt (same as Scene One)
   Tie (same as Scene One)
GINA
   Blouse (same as Scene One)
   Dress (same as Scene One)
EMILY
   Summer dress (same as Scene One)
COLE
   T-shirt (same as Scene One)
   Pants (same as Scene One)

Scene Three

RAYMOND
    Shirt
    Slacks
DUNCAN
    Work shirt (same as Scene One)
    Pants (same as Scene One)

Scene Four

GINA
    Blouse
    Dress
COLE
    T-shirt (same as Scene One)
    Pants (same as Scene One)
DUNCAN
    Work shirt (same as Scene One)
    Pants (same as Scene One)
EMILY
    Evening dress

Scene Five

RAYMOND
    Suit (same as Scene One)
    Shirt (same as Scene One)
    Tie (same as Scene One)
DUNCAN
    Work shirt (same as Scene One)
    Pants (same as Scene One)
EMILY
    Summer dress (same as Scene One)
COLE
    T-shirt (same as Scene One)
    Pants (same as Scene One)
GINA
    Blouse
    Dress

SOUND EFFECTS

Ocean

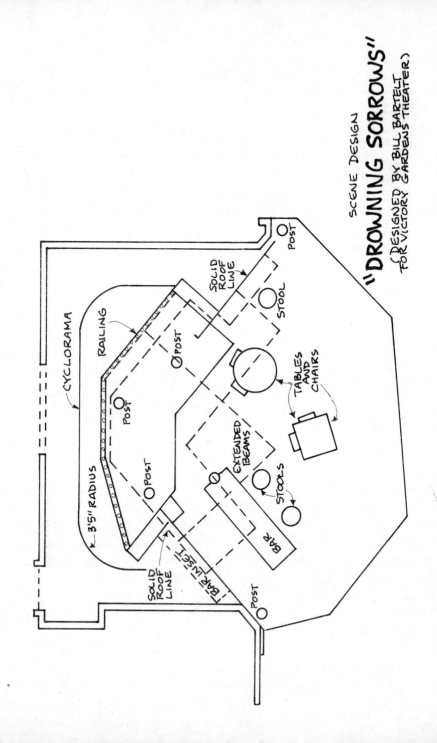

SCENE DESIGN

"DROWNING SORROWS"

(DESIGNED BY BILL BARTELT
FOR VICTORY GARDENS THEATER)

CYCLORAMA

RAILING

SOLID ROOF LINE

POST

STOOL

POST

TABLES AND CHAIRS

3'5" RADIUS

POST

EXTENDED BEAMS

STOOLS

BAR

SOLID ROOF LINE

BAR LINE 1

POST